W9-CFQ-356

How To Convince Your Parents You Can...

Care For A Pet Bunny

Susan Sales Harkins and
William H. Harkins

P.O. Box 196
Hockessin, Delaware 19707
Visit us on the web: www.
Comments? email us: mitchelllane@mi

Printing   1   2   3   4   5   6   7   8   9

A Robbie Reader/How to Convince Your Parents You Can...

Care for a Pet Bunny
Care for a Pet Chameleon
Care for a Pet Chimpanzee
Care for a Pet Ferret
Care for a Pet Horse

Care for a Pet Mouse
Care for a Pet Snake
Care for a Pet Tarantula
Care for a Potbellied Pig
Care for a Wild Chincoteague Pony

Library of Congress Cataloging-in-Publication Data
Harkins, Susan Sales.
   Care for a pet bunny / by Susan Sales Harkins and William H. Harkins.
      p. cm. — (A Robbie Reader—How to convince your parents you can...)
   Includes bibliographical references and index.
   ISBN 978-1-58415-659-8 (library bound)
   1. Rabbits—Juvenile literature. I. Harkins, William H. II. Title.
   SF453.2.H37 2008
   636.932'2—dc22
                              2008002239

ABOUT THE AUTHORS: Susan and William Harkins live in Kentucky, where they enjoy writing together for children. Susan has written many books for adults and children. William is a history buff. In addition to writing, he is a member of the Air National Guard.

PHOTO CREDITS: Cover, pp. 1, 3, 4, 7, 12—JupiterImages; pp. 8, 11, 16, 17, 28, 29—Dan and Jennifer Grande of Perrysburg Rabbits; p. 18—Susan Harkins; p. 21—Martha Martin and Brian Tankersley of The Rabbit Tank; p. 24—Gerry Scarfe.

   Special thanks to Dan Grande for all his help with this book.

TABLE OF CONTENTS

Chapter One 5
Rabbits Are Everywhere

Chapter Two 9
Choose the Right Rabbit

Chapter Three 13
Find the Right Rabbit

Chapter Four 19
Bringing Your Rabbit Home

Chapter Five 25
Still Want a Rabbit?

Find Out More 29
  Books 29
  Works Consulted 29
  On the Internet 29
  Sanctuaries and Rescues 30
Glossary 31
Index 32

Words in **bold** type can be found in the glossary.

Hares are one type of wild rabbit. Hares don't make good pets, and you should never try to pick one up.

RABBITS ARE EVERYWHERE

Your parents might be surprised to learn that you want a pet rabbit. "You're not bringing a rat into this house!" your mom might screech. Some people think rabbits are **rodents** (ROH-dents), but they are wrong. Rabbits belong to the order Lagomorph (LAA-guh-morf), which also includes hares and pikas (PY-kuz).

Rabbits, hares, and pikas all have fur and short fluffy tails. They are herbivores (UR-buh-vorz), which means they eat only plants. Wild rabbits live almost everywhere on earth. They live in deserts, forests, grasslands, and wetlands.

These three creatures aren't the same in every way. Most important, only rabbits make good pets. In nature, rabbits live in holes in the ground called warrens. They are good diggers, which can get them into trouble when they live indoors as pets. A baby

rabbit is called a kit, or kitten. At first, their eyes are closed and they have no fur.

Hares are larger than rabbits. Their long ears stand straight up. They nest on the ground in hollow spots called forms. A baby hare is called a leveret (LEH-vuh-ret). Leverets are born with fur and open eyes.

fun FACTS

Wild rabbits have good hearing, so they can tell when danger is coming their way.

Pikas are the smallest of the three. They have short ears and build haystacks in which to live.

For thousands of years, people have eaten rabbits and used their fur for clothing. Today, we think of rabbits as lovable and gentle pets. Unlike a dog, you don't have to walk a rabbit. Rabbits are friendlier than most cats. Like dogs and cats, they do need love. Your house rabbit will need a lot of attention.

You'll know your rabbit is happy if it "goes binky." The rabbit shakes its head from side to side and hops forward. In mid-hop, it kicks its legs sideways.

Even though they can't bark or meow, rabbits can **communicate** (kuh-MYOO-nih-kayt). Your

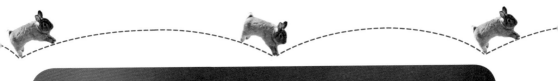

Pikas are related to rabbits, but they don't make good pets. They are shy, and chances are you'll never see one in the wild.

rabbit will bump your foot with its nose when it wants attention. Happy rabbits grind their teeth. When they're calm, they rest on their sides.

Don't expect your rabbit to be happy all the time. Thumping a back foot or shivering means that your rabbit is unhappy or angry. Sometimes a rabbit will even turn its back to you if it's upset. An annoyed rabbit might swish its tail. If your rabbit growls or pushes your hand away, leave it alone for a while.

Your rabbit will need lots of space to run and play. It will require a lot of your time. In return, your rabbit will rub you with its nose, lie close to you on the floor, and make you laugh.

Lop-eared rabbits have long ears that fall to the sides. Those ears require special care, because they get dirty.

Chapter Two

CHOOSE THE RIGHT RABBIT

Don't nag your parents to rush out and buy the first cute rabbit you can find. Learn about the different kinds of rabbits first. They come in many sizes and colors. They have short or long hair. Some have long, straight ears. Others have lop ears that fall to the side.

Some people raise long-haired rabbits for their fur. They brush or comb the rabbit's fur and turn it into soft yarn. Don't worry, it doesn't hurt the rabbit. Someone must brush these rabbits every day. **Lop-eared** rabbits also need special care. You must check and clean their ears often.

Small rabbits tend to be nervous. Large rabbits are heavy and hard to handle. The best rabbit is somewhere in the middle, between 4 and 10 pounds. Some **breeds** make good pets because they are calm and friendly.

The Dutch rabbit weighs 3 1/2 to 5 1/2 pounds. Its face, torso, and front legs are white. Its ears, neck, and hind legs are dark. Dutch rabbits have large, upright ears.

The Mini Lop rabbit weighs 4 1/2 to 6 1/2 pounds. It has lop ears, a fat body, and a short neck. Mini Lops come in many colors. They make some of the best rabbit pets.

The French Lop weighs 10 to 14 pounds and has floppy ears. French Lops come in many colors and make excellent pets.

The New Zealand weighs 9 to 12 pounds and has upright ears. This breed comes in many colors.

The Silver Fox weighs 9 to 12 pounds and has long upright ears. Its fur is silver-white.

Baby rabbits are cute, but they need a lot of care. Sometimes they bite and scratch. Choose an older rabbit that needs a good home if you can.

Rabbits live for a long time. They can get as old as fifteen years. Will you be able to care for a rabbit that long? It's not fair to bring a rabbit home if you can't care for it.

You might think that two rabbits are better than one. In some ways, you'd be right. They will keep each other company if they are already friends. On the other hand, rabbits that don't like each other

Baby bunnies are so cute that they're hard to resist. They're delicate and require more care than a grown rabbit.

fight. If you get a girl, called a **doe**, and a boy, called a **buck**, you will end up with lots of babies. Most likely, that will not please your parents. Where would you find good homes for them?

Don't pick a rabbit because it's cute and cuddly. Choose a rabbit with a good personality. Most mixed breeds, the New Zealand, the Mini Lop, and the French Lop make good pets.

Mixed-breed rabbits are the most common, and often, they make the best pets.

 **Chapter Three** **3**

FIND THE RIGHT RABBIT

There are many types of rabbits. Some need more care than others. A pet rabbit doesn't need to be a fancy or expensive **breed**. In fact, special breeds don't always make good pets.

Start your search at your local animal shelter. A rejected bunny often makes the best pet because it's so glad to have a loving home. Rabbits usually end up in shelters because their owners didn't learn how to take care of them. You can also find rabbit rescue groups online. These groups have lots of rabbits that are waiting for good homes.

Breeders raise rabbits to sell. Most breeders, but not all, love their rabbits. Look for clean cages and healthy rabbits. Each rabbit should have fresh water and clean bedding. Don't purchase a rabbit that is **skittish** (SKIH-tish). Don't buy one that huddles in a corner of its cage.

Pet store rabbits are usually expensive. Sometimes, they're not healthy. Employees don't always know about rabbits. They might give you the wrong sex or even the wrong breed. Ask lots of questions. If you buy your rabbit at a pet store, ask for a **guarantee** (gar-un-TEE).

Once you find a rabbit, ask to hold it. Check it over carefully. Its eyes should be bright, clear, and clean. Make sure the rabbit is clean and its nose is dry. Healthy rabbits have shiny, soft fur. Check its hind legs for bald spots. Its upper and lower teeth should meet. They should not stick out of its mouth. A rabbit that is bucktoothed like Bugs Bunny can't eat and will die.

In the end, the choice might not be yours. A rabbit might choose you. One rabbit might be more interested in you than all the others. If that happens, that rabbit might just be your rabbit!

*fun*FACTS

There are over 150 different rabbit coat colors, but only 5 eye colors (brown, blue-gray, blue, marbled, and pink).

YOU'LL NEED MANY THINGS FOR YOUR NEW RABBIT

A roomy cage
A smaller traveling cage
Two litter boxes
A special scoop for cleaning litter
Food and water dishes (or a water bottle)
Food, including hay and **pellets** (PEL-etz)
Toys

The main cage must be big enough for a litter box and dishes, and still have room for your rabbit to move around. The following size guidelines should help:

Rabbits 2 to 4 pounds need a cage that's
    1 1/2 feet by 2 1/2 feet.
Rabbits 4 to 8 pounds need a cage that's
    2 feet by 3 feet.
Rabbits 8 to 12 pounds need a cage that's
    2 feet by 4 feet.
Rabbits 12 pounds or more need a cage that's
    3 feet by 5 feet.

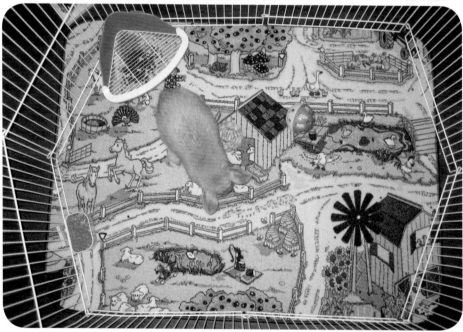

Rabbit cages should be large enough for the rabbit to move around easily. When you want to let it out, you can put your rabbit in a penned area where it will have room to run and play.

Rabbits get bored easily. Give them plenty of toys to keep them busy and happy.

If the entire floor is wire, cover part of it with wood, cardboard, or a mat so that the rabbit can rest comfortably. Some cages come with bands of steel, called urine (YUR-en) guards, around the bottom. These keep the rabbit from spraying urine on nearby walls and the floor. That will make your parents happy.

Lexie properly holds her bunny, Cupcake. It's important to hold a rabbit close. Some rabbits will jump if they're scared. Cup the rabbit's hind end in one hand. Use your other hand to hold the rabbit's front paws and head.

BRINGING YOUR RABBIT HOME

Before you bring your new rabbit home, set up its cage. Find a place to put the cage that is away from heat vents, stoves, fireplaces, drafts, and windows. Don't put the cage too close to a television set or stereo. Rabbits don't like loud noises. Never leave a rabbit in direct sunlight, whether indoors or outdoors. Most important, find a spot where the rabbit can spend lots of time with your family. Rabbits enjoy company.

Put one litter box in the cage and one in the room where your rabbit will play every day. Check with pet and feed stores for special rabbit litter, or use shredded paper. Don't use cat litter or cedar shavings because they might make your rabbit sick. Buy heavy **crockery** (KRAH-kuh-ree) dishes that the rabbit can't knock over.

Buy food pellets that are 14 to 18 percent protein, 20 to 25 percent fiber, and about 2 percent fat for adult rabbits. Growing rabbits have special needs. Some experts say young rabbits need more protein, as much as 20 percent. Other experts recommend less. Check with your

Rabbits can see behind themselves without turning their head.

veterinarian (veh-truh-NAY-ree-un) for the best advice for your rabbit. If your rabbit suddenly stops eating its food, throw away the remaining food and buy a new bag. The food might be spoiled.

Put timothy hay in the cage for bedding and food. Rabbits should always have plenty of fresh hay. It is an important part of their diet.

Let a baby rabbit eat as many pellets as it wants. At six months, feed your rabbit one-third cup per day for each 5 pounds. For instance, if your rabbit weighs 10 pounds, feed it two-thirds cup per day. A rabbit that weighs 7 pounds needs about a half cup of food each day. After a year, feed your rabbit a quarter cup per day for each 5 pounds that it weighs. Some rabbits, such as Angoras, require more food, so check with your veterinarian.

Dot, a Netherland Dwarf bunny, tickles her owner, Garron, with kisses. Some rabbits don't like to be picked up or held, but many do. Your rabbit will let you know what it likes.

Rabbits also need fresh vegetables and fruit. Wash and dry a variety of vegetables every day. Chop them into small pieces.

Don't feed fresh vegetables to baby rabbits (under three months old). Once your rabbit is three months old, you may offer it fresh vegetables. Offer only a few bites of one vegetable at a time. If something upsets your rabbit's stomach, don't feed it to your rabbit anymore. About once a week, add a few bites of a new vegetable. Gradually increase its

DAILY	TREATS	NEVER
alfalfa sprouts, brussels sprouts, carrot tops, parsley, cilantro, dark green leaf lettuce, radish, mustard greens, asparagus, basil, watercress, squash, pumpkin leaves, radish tops, clover, peppers	carrots, celery, parsnips, kale, peas, spinach, collard greens, chicory greens, broccoli	iceberg lettuce, raw beans, raw potatoes, onions, sweet corn
apple (no stem or seeds), blueberries, melon, papaya, peach, pear, pineapple, plum, strawberries	banana, grapes, raisins	

vegetables as it grows. At six months, your rabbit needs 2 cups of vegetables and 2 tablespoons of fresh fruit for every 5 pounds of rabbit, every day. That's a lot of chopping!

Keep in mind that too many raw vegetables will give your rabbit gas. Sugary treats, grains, and nuts are bad for your rabbit.

Twice a day, give your rabbit half its pellet food and vegetables. Always feed your rabbit in the morning before you go to school and again in the early evening. Try to feed your rabbit at the same time every day.

Your rabbit should visit the veterinarian shortly after you bring it home, and then once a year for a checkup. Your vet will tell you about the **vaccinations** (vak-sih-NAY-shunz) and other medical care your rabbit will need.

If your rabbit stops eating and playing or if its droppings don't look normal, you must take it to the veterinarian. Some other signs that mean you should take your bunny to the vet include: sniffles, weepy eyes, long teeth, head shaking, scabs in the ears, and leaning to one side.

All rabbits like to play. Give your rabbit the cardboard center from a roll of paper towels. Fill an old tissue box or brown paper bag with shredded newspaper. Your rabbit will spend hours chewing an old phonebook to shreds. Give it untreated pine blocks to chew. Rabbits like to toss baby toys made out of hard plastic. They enjoy pushing around plastic balls made for cats. They will chew on wooden toys made for large parrots. They will enjoy shredding an untreated willow basket. Make sure your rabbit has plenty of toys and attention to keep it happy and out of trouble.

Kelsey holds Huckleberry, an Angora rabbit. After Huckleberry is combed, he will look only half as big. The fur that is gathered by combing will be spun into yarn. Besides being useful, Angora rabbits are lovable pets.

Chapter Five **5**

STILL WANT A RABBIT?

Almost all rabbits can be good pets. There's a lot for you and your parents to consider. Most important, rabbits need a lot of time, patience, and love. They often don't like to be picked up, but most like to be petted. Rabbits do best when you keep the same routine each day. Strangers may upset your rabbit. Yours will let you know what it likes.

All rabbits love to play. An ignored rabbit is an unhappy rabbit. An unhappy rabbit usually dies.

Rabbits aren't good pets for very young children. Small children are too rough and can hurt a rabbit. Rabbits will bite if they're mad or scared.

Never leave your rabbit alone with a cat or dog. Rabbits don't like ferrets. Reptiles carry **salmonella** (sal-muh-NEL-uh), which kills rabbits.

Perhaps the biggest problem is their droppings. Older rabbits will use a litter box, but they will still

leave a few droppings on the floor to mark their **territory** (TAYR-ih-tor-ee). Young rabbits simply forget to use a litter box.

Rabbits have an odd habit of eating their droppings. Although it seems gross to us, don't stop your rabbit from doing this. The droppings contain special **nutrients** (NOO-tree-entz) that the rabbit needs. Warn your parents so they'll understand why your rabbit does this.

You must **spay** (SPAY) or **neuter** (NOO-ter) your rabbit. If you don't, your rabbit might spray the house with urine. If that happens, your parents might make you get rid of your rabbit.

Rabbits like to chew everything. They will chew your furniture, rugs, shoes, and even electrical cords. You can purchase special wrap for cords at most electronics stores, but your rabbit will **gnaw** (NAW) on the wrap, so you must check it often. Replace gnawed covers. These coverings protect the rabbit and the cord. Keep things off the floor when the rabbit is out. Sometimes that isn't enough, because some rabbits can climb.

Make sure your parents know that rabbits need attention every day. You will need their help. Also, keeping a pet rabbit will increase your food bill. Rabbits need a lot of fresh vegetables every day. You'll have to clean, chop, and feed these vegetables

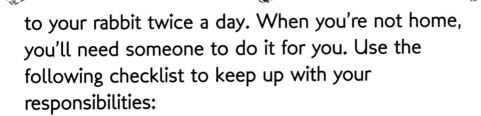

to your rabbit twice a day. When you're not home, you'll need someone to do it for you. Use the following checklist to keep up with your responsibilities:

EVERY DAY	Let your rabbit out to play every morning. Remove dirty litter from both litter boxes. Sweep the cage clean of droppings and spilled food. Make sure your rabbit's droppings look healthy. Use white vinegar to wipe up urine in the cage. Remove shredded paper and cardboard. Stock the cage with fresh timothy hay. Give your rabbit fresh water and food. Let your rabbit out to play each evening. How long depends on you and your rabbit, but your rabbit should spend more than an hour out of its cage every single day. Brush or comb your rabbit, but do not bathe it. If you have a lop rabbit, check its ears to make sure they are clean.
ONCE A WEEK	Empty both litter boxes into the trash or onto the compost pile. Wash litter boxes with white vinegar. Fill litter boxes with clean litter. Clean all dishes and water bottles with white vinegar. Remove all the timothy hay and sweep up all droppings and spilled food. Clean plastic toys with white vinegar. Throw away any plastic toy that's chipped or broken.
ONCE A MONTH	Clean everything with a weak bleach solution (one part bleach to ten parts water).
ONCE A YEAR	Visit your veterinarian for vaccinations and a checkup.

REMEMBER: ALWAYS WASH YOUR HANDS AFTER HANDLING LITTER AND HAY AND BEFORE AND AFTER YOU PLAY WITH YOUR RABBIT.

Thunder, a Flemish Giant, waits to be taken for a walk. Rabbits can be trained to walk on a leash, just like a dog. A harness will work better than a collar on your rabbit. Remember not to leave your rabbit in direct sunlight while you're outside.

A happy rabbit needs your love and attention, but that's not all. You still have to keep your rabbit out of trouble to keep your rabbit safe and your parents happy. You can do both by playing with your rabbit a lot. If your rabbit is playing with you, it won't chew your mother's favorite shoes or the remote control. More important, your rabbit will be happy and healthy.

FIND OUT MORE

Books

Coppendale, Jean. *You and Your Pet Rabbit.* Irvine, California: QEB Publishing, Inc., 2004.

Head, Honor. *My Pet Rabbit.* Austin, Texas: Raintree Steck-Vaughn Publishers, 2001.

Hibbert, Clare. *Looking After Your Pet Rabbit.* London, United Kingdom: Hodder Wayland, 2003.

Magloff, Lisa. *Watch Me Grow: Rabbit.* New York: DK Publishing, Inc., 2004.

Miller, Sara Swan. *Rabbits, Pikas, and Hares.* New York: Franklin Watts, 2002.

Royston, Angela. *Baby Animals: Rabbit.* North Mankato, Minnesota: Chrysalis Education, 2005.

Whitehouse, Patricia. *Rabbits.* Chicago, Illinois: Heinemann Library, 2004.

Works Consulted

Davis, Susan E., and Margo Demello. *Stories Rabbits Tell.* New York: Lantern Books, 2003.

Gendron, Karen. *The Rabbit Handbook.* Hauppauge, New York: Barron's Educational Series, Inc., 2000.

Moore, Lucile C. *A House Rabbit Primer: Understanding and Caring for Your Companion Rabbit.* Santa Monica, California: Santa Monica Press LLC, 2005.

Pavia, Audrey. *The Rabbit.* New York: Wiley Publishing, Inc., 1996, 2001.

Dan Grande from Perrysburg Rabbits, holding Thunder

On the Internet

Perrysburg Rabbits
http://www.perrysburgrabbits.com

The Rabbit Tank—Online Rabbitry
http://www.rabbittank.com/

Sanctuaries and Rescues

Bright Eyes Sanctuary & Rabbit Rescue
http://brighteyessanctuary.org/

H.A.R.E. (House Rabbit Adoption, Rescue and Education)
http://www.bio.miami.edu/hare/hare.html

House Rabbit Society
http://www.rabbit.org/

How to Care for Rabbits, The Humane Society of the United
States, http://www.hsus.org/pets/pet_care/rabbit_horse_
and_other_pet_care/how_to_care_for_rabbits.html

The Language of Lagomorphs: What Your Rabbit Is Saying and
How to Speak Back
http://www.muridae.com/rabbits/rabbittalk.html

Rabbit Care: The 411, Animaland, ASPCA
http://www.aspca.org/site/PageServer?pagename=kids_pc_
rabbit_411

Rabbit References, Charky & Ash's Web Site
http://homepage.mac.com/mattocks/morfz/rabresc.html

Rabbit Rescue & Rehab, New York City Chapter of the House
Rabbit Society
http://www.rabbitcare.org/

Wild Rescue
http://www.rescuedrabbits.org/

Zooh Corner Rabbit Rescue
http://www.mybunny.org

GLOSSARY

breed (BREED)—Animals of the same species that share the same traits.

breeders (BREED-erz)—People who raise animals for profit or show.

buck (BUK)—A male, or boy, rabbit.

communicate (kuh-MYOO-nih-kayt)—To share feelings and information.

crockery (KRAH-kuh-ree)—Dishes made of dried earth or clay.

doe (DOH)—A female, or girl, rabbit.

gnaw (NAW)—To chew.

guarantee (gar-un-TEE)—To promise that a product is good or money will be returned.

lop-eared (LOP-eerd)—Having ears that droop.

neuter (NOO-ter)—To remove a male's reproductive organs.

nutrients (NOO-tree-entz)—Healthy ingredients.

pellets (PEL-letz)—Small, hard pieces of food.

rodent (ROH-dent)—A gnawing or nibbling mammal.

salmonella (sal-muh-NEL-uh)—A disease of the intestines.

skittish (SKIH-tish)—Easily scared.

spay (SPAY)—To remove a female's reproductive organs.

territory (TAYR-ih-tor-ee)—A stretch of land or region that an animal claims as its own.

vaccinations (vak-sih-NAY-shunz)—Shots that will help your rabbit fight diseases.

veterinarian (vet-ruh-NAYR-ee-un)—An animal doctor.

INDEX

breeders 13

breeds 9, 10, 13, 14
   Angora 20, 24
   Dutch 10
   Flemish Giant 28
   French Lop 10, 11
   lop-eared 8, 9, 10, 11, 27
   Mini Lop 10, 11
   mixed 11, 12
   Netherland Dwarf 21
   New Zealand 10, 11
   Silver Fox 10

bucks 11

cage 13, 15, 16, 17, 19, 20, 27

does 11

hares 4, 5, 6

herbivores 5

kits 6, 11

lagomorphs 5–7

leverets 6

litter box 15, 19, 25–26, 27

pet stores 14

pikas 5, 6, 7

rabbit
   babies 5–6, 10, 11, 20, 21
   diet 5, 20–23
   droppings 23, 25–26, 27
   eyes 6, 14, 23
   fur 5, 6, 9, 10, 14
   going binky 6
   health 13, 14, 23, 27, 28
   holding your 18
   lifespan of 10
   moods 6–7, 13, 21, 25
   and other pets 25
   responsibilities 25–28
   and sunlight 19, 28
   teeth 7, 14, 23
   toys 15, 17, 23, 27
   walking your 28

rodents 5

salmonella 25

vaccinations 23, 27

veterinarian 20, 23, 27

wild rabbits 4, 5–6